SPECTRUM®
READERS

W9-AUE-438

LEVEL 2

INTENSE!
Machines

By Teresa Domnauer

Carson-Dellosa
Publishing

SPECTRUM®

An imprint of Carson-Dellosa Publishing, LLC
P.O. Box 35665
Greensboro, NC 27425-5665

carsondellosa.com

Printed in the USA. All rights reserved.
ISBN 978-1-62399-145-6

01-002131120

Extreme machines do important jobs.
They help people build and explore.
They help people move and travel.
They help people farm and rescue.
They help people have fun, too.

Front-End Loader

This machine is a front-end loader.
You might see one at a building site.
It scoops up huge loads of dirt
with its bucket.
It pours the dirt into a dump truck.

Giant Dump Truck

This machine is a giant dump truck.
You might see one at a mine.
It carries huge loads of soil and rocks
in its bed.
It dumps the load wherever
it is needed.

Combine

This machine is a combine.
You might see one at a farm.
It can pick a whole field
of corn in a day.
It takes the kernels off the corn
and collects them in a bin.

Indy Car

This machine is an Indy car.
You might see one at a racetrack.
It can reach speeds of 200 miles
per hour or more.
It got its name from a famous race—
the Indianapolis 500.

Chopper

This machine is a chopper.
You might see one on the road.
A chopper is a specially built
motorcycle.
It is lighter and faster than most
motorcycles!

Fire Truck

This machine is a fire truck.
You might see one racing
down the street.
It has a ladder that is almost
100 feet long.
The ladder helps firefighters get
to the tops of tall buildings.

Helicopter

This machine is a helicopter.
You might see one flying
over your city.
This kind carries people to the
hospital during an emergency.
Nurses and paramedics ride in it.
They care for the hurt person
during the flight.

Locomotive

This machine is a locomotive.
You might see one zooming
along railroad tracks.
It has a very powerful engine.
It pulls long trains loaded with freight.
It pulls passenger trains, too.

Boeing 747

This machine is a Boeing 747.
You might see one soaring in the sky.
It is a huge jumbo jet
with four engines.
It carries passengers all over the world.
It can even carry a space shuttle
on its back!

Semitruck

This machine is a semitruck.
You might see one on the highway.
It hauls big loads across the country.
Some semitrucks have a bed
behind the driver's seat.
Then, truck drivers can stop and
rest inside.

Cargo Ship

This machine is a cargo ship.
You might see one on the ocean.
It delivers huge amounts of things
all around the world. It carries food,
oil, and many other goods.

Submarine

This machine is a submarine.
You might see one coming up
out of the water.
Its special shape helps it move
smoothly through the water.
Some submarines are used in war.
Others help scientists explore ocean life.

Aircraft Carrier

This machine is an aircraft carrier.
You might see one at a Navy base.
This giant ship carries military planes.
It is so big that planes can take off
and land on its deck.

Space Shuttle

This machine is a space shuttle.
You might see one flying in space.
It blasts off like a rocket,
but it lands like an airplane.
It can be used again and again
for exploring space.

INTENSE! Machines
Comprehension Questions

1. Name two important jobs of extreme machines.

2. Where might you see a front-end loader?

3. What might a giant dump truck carry